Planning Green Growth
a socialist contribution to the debate on environmental sustainability

by Pete Dickenson

Planning Green Growth
a socialist contribution to the debate on environmental sustainability
by Pete Dickenson

First Edition January 2003

ISBN 1-870958 24 1 pbk

Published by CWI Publications and Socialist Books
for the Committee for a Workers International
Designed and typeset by Kavita Graphics
Typeset in Usherwood 9 pt
Printed by Russell Press (Nottingham)

Distribution by Socialist Books
PO Box 24697, London, E11 1YD
Telephone +44 (0)20 8988 8777

typesetting & design: dennis@kavitagraphics.co.uk

Planning Green Growth

a socialist contribution to the debate on environmental sustainability

by Pete Dickenson

This timely new pamphlet analyses the causes and scope of environmental destruction across the globe and asks what is the way forward. The Committee for a Workers International (CWI) is pleased to publish 'Planning Green Growth' which is a personal contribution by Pete Dickenson to the debate on environmental sustainability

The author is a researcher and lecturer in Britain in the fields of environmental management and East European studies, particularly on the impact of the restoration of capitalism on the former Soviet Union. Pete is also a long standing member of the Socialist Party, section of the CWI in England and Wales

1 Introduction

Although the second UN sponsored Earth Summit in South Africa in September 2002 was supposed to develop a programme to avert the environmental crisis looming over the planet, it only produced an empty wish list of aims. The Western powers made it clear in advance that no more money would be available to achieve these aims and it would be up to individual countries whether or not to implement them. On the crucial issue of preventing global warming, it was merely resolved to "substantially increase" the use of renewable energy without any targets being set. Even conservative commentators in the West were forced to admit that the imperialist countries treated the Earth Summit simply as a cheap public relations stunt.

A statement issued by Greenpeace, Oxfam and Friends of the Earth before the meeting in South Africa was sceptical, with good reason as it turned out. It said that it was embarrassing, in the build up to the summit, to see different nations and blocs single-mindedly pursuing their own narrow interests at the expense of poor people and the planet's future. The statement went on: "The system of horse-trading, back-room deals and bullying by powerful blocs is becoming common practice in international negotiations. Rarely has it produced so little by way of firm results. We have been appalled to watch governments renege on commitments made at Rio ten years ago." Although socialists share this scepticism, we think it is necessary to draw all the necessary conclusions that flow from past experience, particularly as regards the role of the capitalist market system in the degradation of the environment and as the main barrier to a sustainable future. It is significant that virtually all the participants in the Earth Summit, including the US, agreed that using capitalist market methods was the only way to avert the environmental crisis facing the world. They differed only on the type of market tools to use, or on the extent that the state should be involved in implementing and policing their operation.

The socialist alternative

When the US administration dumped the Kyoto agreement, which aimed to reduce global warming, millions of environmental activists throughout the world were enraged. The message was loud and clear: that the interests of the multinational corporations - represented by the White House - come before the looming environmental disaster caused by greenhouse gas emissions. President Bush's blatant policy of defending the profits of US companies has brought into question the credibility of international agreements between rival capitalist powers and prompted a debate among left-wing environmentalists about the way forward. A socialist alternative to the destructive anarchy of the market system is needed, which will give a path to environmental sustainability - a term that has been defined as the establishment of conditions for life on earth to continue into the distant future.

According to most environmental activists reducing global warming and other environmental threats to sustainable levels is not just a technical issue, but is closely tied to the question of reducing or reversing economic growth. Since this has great implications for the possibility of abolishing poverty throughout the world, which is a prerequisite for building socialism, a different strategy needs to be explored. An important aspect of this debate, which is only just beginning to be considered, is proposing an alternative to the market system, whose single-minded quest for profit is the prime cause of unsustainable environmental destruction. The collapse of the Soviet Union and the degradation of the environment in Eastern Europe during the Stalinist period appeared to discredit the ideas of planning as an alternative to capitalism. However, the planned use of resources, as compared to the anarchy of 'free enterprise', will be the essential tool in tackling the problem of global warming and other threats. Such a planned economy, if it is democratically controlled, is an alternative both to capitalism and to the perversion of socialism practised in the former USSR.

A social system based on need not profit would have enormous inherent advantages from the viewpoint of saving energy. For instance, it would avoid the duplication of resources, planned obsolescence and wide-scale destruction of factories, plant and machinery in slumps, characteristic of the capitalist profit system. Eliminating these features of the system will have a significant impact in increasing the efficiency of energy usage and therefore reducing pollution. However, the biggest environmental advantage of a socialist society, where production is driven by need not profit, is the ability to tackle the threats facing us using democratic planning, compared to the inevitable environmental degeneration linked to the anarchy of capitalist production.

The developing world economic crisis, perhaps the most serious since the Great Depression, could divert attention from the problems of the environment, because the output of some forms of pollution will temporarily fall, along with the decline in economic activity. However, the history of capitalism shows that after even a deep crisis, with its resulting suffering and devastation, a recovery eventually occurs and a new phase of unplanned anarchic growth ensues, leading to a further twist in the spiral of environmental degeneration.

2 The nature of the problem

Few, except for George Bush and his carefully picked 'experts' who speak for the interests of the oil companies and other multinationals, argue against the view that we face an impending environmental crisis. So, while it is not necessary here to prove that a catastrophe is looming over us - the evidence is now compelling - it is useful to give a quick summary of the key threats in order to put the arguments about sustainability into context.

The main symptoms and causes of unsustainability are summarised in table 1. To eliminate the effects of all these symptoms will be a massive task, something the anarchy of the capitalist market has been incapable of getting to grips with. All the factors shown in Table 1 pose major threats to sustainability and many of them are linked to each other. For instance, deforestation contributes to global warming because the reduced amount of vegetation is no longer able to absorb as much

Table 1. Symptoms and causes of environmental unsustainability

Symptoms	Main Causes
Pollution	
Greenhouse effect/climate change	Emissions of Carbon Dioxide, CFCs and Methane
Nuclear waste contamination	Production of nuclear reactor by-products
Ozone depletion	Emissions of CFCs
Acidification	Emissions of sulphur dioxide and nitrous oxide
Non-nuclear toxic contamination	Sulphur dioxide, nitrous oxide and ozone
Renewable resource depletion	
Species extinction	Land use changes, future climate change and ozone depletion.
Deforestation	Land use changes, future climate change
Land degradation	Unsustainable agricultural methods
Fishery destruction	Overfishing, habitat destruction
Non-renewable resource depletion	
Depletion of various resources	Extraction and use of minerals and fossil fuels

carbon dioxide, the major greenhouse gas. There is not space to describe all the headings in the table, but three of the most intractable and difficult areas - the greenhouse effect, nuclear waste contamination and ozone depletion - need some further explanation in order to understand the scale of the crisis.

Greenhouse effect

The greenhouse effect is where certain gases (e.g. carbon dioxide - CO_2) in the earth's atmosphere are more transparent to the short-wave radiation from the sun than the longer-wave re-radiation from the earth's surface. The result is that some of the heat from the sun is trapped inside the atmosphere, a similar effect to that occurring in a greenhouse. The greater the concentration of greenhouse gases such as carbon dioxide, the more heat is trapped and the tendency for the average temperature of the earth's surface to go up is established.

Since the industrial revolution began over 200 years ago, CO_2 levels have increased by about 25% and the concentration of methane, another greenhouse gas, has more than doubled. CFCs, the gases released by aerosol sprays, are also major contributors to greenhouse gas (GG) emissions, although their contribution is likely to slowly fall due to the very belated international government actions to phase them out. The effects of the rise in emissions of GGs have still to be experienced, but the potential for disaster is clearly there. The Intergovernmental Panel on Climate Change (IPCC) has estimated that sea levels could rise by up to one metre this century. This would devastate the inhabitants of the flood plains of Bangladesh and Egypt, and worldwide hundreds of millions of the very poor would be displaced. Extending the prediction of the IPCC to 250 years gives a sea level rise of up to four metres (12 feet), which would make significant areas of the earth's surface uninhabitable, including large parts of north-west Europe.

Even these figures are probably conservative since they were based on data drawn up in the 1980s. There is much evidence that global warming is accelerating shown by the fact that the three hottest years since records began in the 1860s occurred in the 1990s. The IPCC calculated that CO2 output must fall by 60% to stabilise the situation, whereas it is was growing at 0.5% in 1992. (The current economic crisis will probably lead to a small decline but this will not alter the long-term trend.)

Nuclear waste contamination

Sections of the capitalist class realise that a climate change disaster is looming and are looking desperately for a cheap way to solve the problem. An answer from their point of view would be to expand nuclear power, since the technology exists, is relatively cheap and does not produce GGs. It would be completely wrong to assume, however, that this option does not pose a serious threat to environmental sustainability, in particular linked to the problem of toxic waste.

A direct consequence of producing electricity with nuclear reactors is the accumulation of radioactive waste, uranium and plutonium. There is also a significant amount of plutonium produced for military purposes which has to be stored. Taking the example of the waste stored in the USA in 1991, it comprised of 4,900 cubic metres with a radioactivity of 24,000 MCi. (A Curie is a unit of radioactivity, MCi is one million Curies.) To get a measure of this figure, a typical radioactive source used in a classroom for a science experiment has an activity of one millionth of a Curie.

An average sized 1,000 megawatt (MW - one million watts) nuclear power station reactor has a total radioactivity of 70 MCi in its spent fuel one year after discharge. After 100,000 years this figure will fall naturally to 2,000 Ci, still two billion times more radioactive than the typical source used in the classroom mentioned above.

The implication of this data is that a safe storage method must be found that can be guaranteed to be secure for more than 100,000 years, a task which poses huge uncertainties and problems because it is difficult to predict what natural conditions will be after that time. If the material is buried, the onset of earthquakes in previously unaffected areas is possible, as is a meteor strike. If the radioactive spent fuel is put at the bottom of the sea the integrity of the materials used as a storage medium must be uncertain after such a long time, possibly leading to seepage. Also undersea volcanic activity could start, producing the same result.

The technical difficulties and understandable opposition from local communities where it has been proposed to dump the wastes, have meant that there will be at least another ten years delay before any supposedly safe site is ready in the USA and another 20 in Europe. In the meantime, the dangers go unchecked, shown by the clusters of child leukaemia cases occurring in the vicinity of the current British nuclear waste storage site at Sellafield.

Ozone depletion

The layer of ozone gas in the atmosphere protects humans and the ecosystem from the harmful effects of the sun's radiation. It has been damaged by the release into the atmosphere of CFCs, which was a chemical used to propel aerosol sprays and also occurs in packing materials. The Montreal Protocol was designed to cut and eventually eliminate the production of CFCs and has had some effect since their output fell by 77% between 1988 and 1994. This may appear a successful example of international capitalist co-operation. In reality the USA held back for years against the Montreal Protocol and only signed up when it was clear that US corporations had taken the lead in developing alternative aerosol propellants.

The result of the delay is that the full recovery of the ozone layer will not take place until the 22nd century, because there is a long delay before the levels of chlorine, in the stratosphere, produced by the CFCs, will start to decline. This means that the benefit of the first reductions in CFCs that took place in the 1980s will not be apparent until 2005. In the meantime, the ozone layer will continue to be destroyed. The 3% loss of ozone noted in 1991 over the USA was expected to produce 12 million extra skin cancers in that country alone.

The scale of the problem

The scale of the environmental threats facing us needs to be understood so that the difficulty in mitigating and then eliminating them can be estimated. The solution to the issue of nuclear waste storage will require huge resources to find a safe method of disposal. Even though governments around the world currently have no answers, they continue to pour out more and more toxic waste, content to leave the problem to future generations. The depletion of the ozone layer is a question of coping for a 100 years with the effects of a 20th century disaster, a legacy of the 'free-market' system. Although nuclear waste disposal and ozone depletion both pose a threat to our long-term future, ranging in time from 100-100,000 years, the question of global warming is potentially even more serious. One expert warned: "Human induced global warming, then, could possibly start a chain reaction of events that could lead to the extinction of civilization or even humanity. This is a remote possibility, but it exists". (Counting the Cost of Global Warming', by J

Broome, White Horse Press, Cambridge, 1992.)

All economic activity requires from the environment raw materials and energy as factor inputs, and an ability to deal with wastes and maintain a global balance (e.g. in surface temperature). Although these functions have been under pressure since the mass production of commodities ushered in the modern capitalist epoch over 200 years ago, only recently has evidence emerged that they are breaking down completely.

Reducing environmental intensity is the key factor in trying to deal with the polluting effects of increased consumption. Environmental intensity is the pollution produced per unit of consumption (e.g. the amount of CO_2 produced in making a tonne of steel) and it has been suggested that there are three ways a reduction in its value can be achieved. The first is changing the composition of output to less damaging products. The second is to substitute harmful economic inputs such as fossil fuels with renewable energy sources. And the last is to develop new technology to increase the efficiency of the use of resources. A fourth possibility is to decrease environmental intensity by changing not just the technical aspects of production but also the social, an issue that will be explored later.

It has been calculated that the impact on the environment resulting from all sources of pollution must be reduced by 50% to ensure sustainable growth. This means that environmental intensity must be reduced by more than ten times if it assumed that consumption and population increase significantly. Detailed calculations are given in the Appendix. (Some environmental groups, such as Friends of the Earth, put the needed reduction in environmental intensity up to five times higher than that stated above.)

3 Is sustainable growth possible on a capitalist basis?

Most capitalist politicians now pay lip service to sustainability, so what are the prescriptions they are proposing to achieve this? Before considering the solutions put forward by the neo-liberal theorists, it is worth emphasising further the scale of the task they are facing. On the crucial question of global warming, the US Department of Energy estimated in 1998 that the cost of cutting CO2 emissions to 7% below their 1990 levels would rise to 4% of US gross domestic product (GDP) by 2010, or in money terms, $400 billion per year. Although this figure is certainly exaggerated as a result of scare-mongering by the US energy lobby (other calculations put comparable GDP figures rising to 1-3% after a much longer time), the very large scale of costs is clear, and would lead to massive tax rises for the multi-nationals.

Property rights

The classic method put forward by the neo-liberal school to take account of environmental damage is the so-called 'property rights' approach, which relies on direct negotiations between the parties affected to resolve the issue. This requires that the property rights to the use of environmental resources are defined and owned by someone. Capitalist commentators generally, and especially neo-liberals, always emphasise the sacrosanct nature of private property, which explains why this is their preferred approach. (Private property is defined here as the means production i.e. factories and so on, and not as the personal property of the individual workers.) However, it is easy to see the practical difficulties in implementing this scheme. For instance, it is hard to see what system of private ownership could be imposed on the stratosphere. Even if it was, the number of people affected by its malfunctioning runs into billions, all of whom could seek redress from the owner, making the method unworkable.

Tradable permits

This practical difficulty in using the property rights approach has even struck some die-hard free-marketeers and an alternative system based on controlling pollution through the price mechanism has been worked out - the so-called 'make the polluter pay' principle. The preferred route this takes is by the trading of pollution permits, issued by a government at a price reflecting the environmental costs and covering a specific geographical area. Leaving aside for the moment the fiasco of the Kyoto permit trading experience, it is not difficult to see that this scheme would be ineffective. For instance, the cost of building flood defences in Bangladesh in 20 years time, needed because of global warming due to emissions by US corporations today, would not be included in the permit price, meaning that the polluter is not really paying at all.

Eco-taxes

An alternative to the permit system is the introduction of an eco-tax, although this is regarded as a dangerously 'socialist' idea by the neo-liberals, compared to the free trading of permits. However, far from being socialist, eco-taxes are reactionary, hitting the poorest hardest since they spend a much greater proportion of their income on energy costs and, at the same time, are hit unfairly by a flat rate tax. This regressive effect will apply to congestion charges, such as those proposed by the London mayor, Ken Livingstone, in an attempt to cut traffic congestion.

The principle of eco-taxes is that increasing the price of polluting resources will create an incentive to use them less and seek substitutes. Evidence to show this works is put forward by comparing the experience of the USA with some other advanced capitalist countries. Energy prices in the US are a third of those in countries like Norway, whereas their emissions of carbon are about three times greater per unit of GDP, thus the tax mechanism seems to work. (The North, the South and the Environment Edited by V Bhaskar and A Glynn, Earthscan, 1995.)

The issue is not so simple, however, when examined in more detail. France, for instance, has a relatively good greenhouse gas performance because it introduced nuclear power on a massive scale which, purely coincidentally, does not produce greenhouse gases. This was done for political reasons, not because the price of fossil fuel was high, therefore questioning the link between high fossil fuel cost and low pollution emission. Also, the evidence shows that key economic factors that help create sustainability, e.g. the development of new non-polluting technology, would not be promoted to a significant extent by adjusting prices through eco-taxes.

Even if taxes could play some role in reducing pollution, there is the question of scale to be considered. The cost to the US for significant cuts in greenhouse gases, given earlier at $400 billion per year, shows that for such a programme to be effective tax increases would have to be huge, more than 100% according to some estimates. This would devastate the profits of big business and make them politically impossible to impose. It is significant that in Scandinavian countries where some form of eco-tax has been implemented, companies are specifically excluded from paying and the whole burden is put on individuals.

Cost-benefit analysis

Cost-benefit analysis (CBA) is a tool that has been used to assess environmental risks and to reach a rational decision, its supporters say, about future investment by giving values to different environmental effects using a common measure, i.e. money. Costs and benefits that will fall on future generations are discounted at an agreed percentage rate to arrive at a 'net present value'. In this way, values can be easily compared and an objective balance of costs and benefits created. Its success however, depends on defining clearly what the costs and benefits are and for all the parties involved to agree on these definitions. Where profit is at stake this is easier said than done.

In capitalist terms, risks must be expressed in money values and probabilities of future adverse events clearly determined. For instance, in one CBA of global warming, the number of deaths that could result due to climate change in the future was estimated. This calculated that 22,923 people would die in the advanced capitalist countries and 114,804 (both very conservative figures) in the rest of the world. The next stage in the CBA was to put a money value on these lives, which resulted in a figure of $1,480,000 per 'advanced capitalist' citizen and $131,000 for each other person. It is hard to see the result of this type of analysis becoming the basis of a mutual agreement based on justice and fairness. When this cannot be done, which is the usual case, environmental risks are effectively ignored by using a system of ordinary discounting.

Using this method, it has been calculated that the cost of a nuclear accident, 500 years in the future and costing £10 billion at current prices to future generations, would be 25 pence, discounted at 5%. In other words, if a CBA was made now about building such a power station, 25 pence would go in the costs column to allow for a future accident. Looking at the question another way round, if a compensation fund were created now to meet the costs of this future accident, it would be necessary to invest only 25p to raise the required sum due to the workings of compound interest over such a long period. The net present cost is clearly dependent on the interest rate used but there is no agreement on what it should be. This is not surprising since it is difficult to predict interest rates five weeks in advance, never mind 500 years.

One expert said: "Through the choice of appropriate parameter values almost any (environmental) abatement policy can be justified." (Source: 'Ekins', 2000.)

Constraints on capitalism

All these capitalist theories to achieve sustainability - property rights, tradable permits or eco-taxes - remain just that, theories. The reasons why none of them have ever been implemented on any significant scale are much more important than the individual criticisms that can be made of each. The thinking elements of the capitalist class internationally realise that an abyss is looming, so why can't they take really decisive action?

The central contradiction of capitalism, from the beginning of the 20th century till the present day, has been its inability to resolve the conflicting needs of profit-driven production and the continuing existence of nation states. In their quest for profit, the capitalists are forced to look for new markets beyond their borders as their own market becomes saturated, bringing them into conflict with rivals from other countries who are under similar pressures. In abstract terms, the rivals could co-operate to more efficiently exploit the rest of the world if the market was continually expanding. But this is never the case for long with capitalism as bust always follows boom. When the market turns down, the tensions grow between the international rivals, and the big corporations look once more to their own governments to protect their profits. This cycle will occur again soon as the drive to globalisation is undermined by the developing downturn.

Any genuine solution to the environmental crisis must be international since all the main threats, such as global warming, ozone depletion, or nuclear toxic waste contamination, affect the entire earth or large parts of it. However, the main capitalist countries that account for the majority of pollution will never meaningfully co-operate if the profits of 'their' multinationals are significantly affected. This is particularly true in a recession, and is the problem that lies at the heart of the environmental crisis.

Kyoto

The fiasco over the Kyoto agreement is a good example to demonstrate the inability of the capitalist system to tackle the crisis. Kyoto intended to tackle global warming by cutting greenhouse gas emissions by a small amount, back to the 1990 level, in itself a modest target. The justification was that this was the maximum that was politically feasible, but even this tiny and cheap step forward, proposed at a time of economic boom, proved to be totally unacceptable to the USA. The agreement was fixed so that no actual reductions in greenhouse gases in the advanced capitalist countries (ACCs) were called for. Instead, a system of tradable permits was introduced, the preferred 'free market' mechanism where ACCs could buy the rights to pollute from other countries that were below their quota. This was possible because, very conveniently, the base year from which calculations were made was 1990, just before the economic slump in the former Soviet Union and

Eastern Europe caused their greenhouse gas output to fall by 50%. This meant that East European states had a large 'surplus' of tradable permits to sell to the ACCs, probably at very reasonable prices considering their desperate plight.

Why did the US Congress vote virtually unanimously to reject this almost completely cosmetic deal? It was probably not because the immediate price was unacceptable since they had reached an agreement, although belated, on the ozone issue that incurred costs to US companies. It was because they regarded this as the thin end of the wedge where, eventually, meaningful cuts would have to be made. Since the US produces 25% of all greenhouse gases, almost twice as much as its principal rivals in the EU, its profits would be disproportionately hit by meaningful cuts. The lesson here is that if small sacrifices only are needed, and they can be evenly distributed between rival capitalists as in the case of CFC reductions, then limited agreements can be made (although it is doubtful that even this would apply in conditions of recession or slump). However, if profits are seriously under threat, then even limited agreement is impossible. This particularly applies if the dominant world power, the USA, is the biggest potential loser.

Direct state intervention

Direct state intervention to reduce pollution, although still operating within the framework of a market-driven society, has been largely discarded as an option by the currently dominant neo-liberal alchemists who dismissively label it 'command and control'. Nonetheless, some pro-capitalist commentators are beginning to reconsider this attitude because they think direct intervention may actually work, in contrast to neo-liberal theorising. A strategy that they propose is to impose a legally enforceable set of standards to control emissions. Other options could also include more radical measures, such as redirecting production to non-polluting sectors, restricting consumer choice to eco-friendly products or prescribing that energy should be produced by renewable sources.

As the environmental crisis deepens, the attractiveness of this approach will grow, particularly to those on the left or active in the green movement who can see the impotence of purely market-based ideas. Although state intervention could have an effect if it was applied in all the major polluting countries in a large-scale manner over the long-term, the question is: will it be? It is possible that an individual country will begin to implement small-scale environmentally-friendly measures, such as in Germany now, or in Scandinavia. However, as soon as the level of investment by the state threatens profits through higher taxes, as it must if the measures are to be sufficiently large-scale to be effective, the big companies will scream that their international competitiveness is being undermined. Since, in the context of capitalism, the priority of the government of each country is to protect the interests of the multi-national companies based inside its borders, any meaningful environmental programme will then be dropped.

The requirement to solve the crisis through international agreements capable of tackling the scale of the problem, remains the same, as do the reasons why they will not happen.

New technology

Although it is theoretically possible that the bacon will be pulled out of the environmental fire by a fortuitous new invention - for example, a technology like nuclear fusion that promised to produce large quantities of energy cheaply and without pollution - there is nothing viable on the horizon. The market system has been unable to provide the scientific breakthroughs that are needed. One of the reasons is that under monopoly capitalism, new technology is the result of long-term incremental advances by teams of scientists and engineers working for multinational corporations where changing course to a radically different direction is very difficult due to their bureaucractic structures. Furthermore, the huge costs of developing the new approaches that are needed in the energy field deter most companies from entering the market. Also, since the lure of profit is still ultimately the reason for investment in new technology, it will be introduced in those sectors that are most profitable in the short and medium term, i.e. for fossil fuel technology rather than renewable energy generation.

Sustainable growth on a capitalist basis is not feasible, partly because the methods it can employ to achieve this are inadequate and flawed, but mainly because imperialist rivalry will prevent the international co-operation that is essential to make progress. The result is that the world will continue to hurtle headlong to disaster since the environment will still be treated as a 'free good' by the multinationals that dominate production and will be exploited at virtually no cost to themselves.

4 The green movement agenda for sustainability

There are many variations of the green and environmental movement agenda, so any categorisation must be approximate and recognise that there is overlap between them. Bearing this in mind, it is still possible to identify three basic trends or approaches. The first two are models based on market solutions, albeit with significant state involvement. The third is sometimes called 'eco-socialist', where market forces are not the dominating feature.

The 'mainstream' market approach asserts the central need for a 'steady-state' economy. Steady state was defined by its initial proponent and guru, Hermann Daly, as fixing absolute limits both to human population and to the 'population of artefacts' (goods). The question of population control is controversial but putting a limit to the production of goods is a common feature of most green policies. The programme of the Green Party in Britain includes import/export controls, control on multinationals through exchange controls, control on speculation through the Tobin tax, limits on the size of monopolies and tax breaks for new small firms entering the market. At the centre of the programme though is a complex system of eco-taxes and permits to encourage environmentally-friendly behaviour which, it is claimed, will lay the basis for a steady state economy.

What would be the implications of a steady-state economy? If steady-state is defined as zero consumption growth from present levels, a 66% reduction in environmental intensity would be needed for sustainability. This assumes the widely predicted large population increase in the 'South' and a small one in the 'North'. However, if it is true, as most greens believe, that this level of reduction in environmental intensity is not feasible, then consumption will have to fall to close the gap. If consumption must decline, what implications does this have for the green programme to redistribute the 'surplus' from the North to the South to establish a fair and equal world? If we assume, on the grounds of fairness and equality, that cuts are limited to the main polluters in the industrialised countries, consumption per head will have to be reduced significantly. In these circumstances the scope for redistributing the industrialised countries' 'surplus' consumption to the rest of the world would be very limited since it would have shrunk enormously. This is true with steady-state as defined here - zero consumption growth. Most greens actually advocate a cut in consumption, which would reduce the surplus even further.

Greens correctly make the point that definitions of consumption are based on calculations of gross national product (GNP) that are boosted by the costs of clearing up environmental damage. The argument goes that, since growth in GNP is a policy objective of all governments, there is no incentive to cut pollution, because the pollution itself is contributing to GNP growth. The conclusion drawn is that, if the definition of GNP is changed to eliminate this effect, governments will change growth policy in an environmentally-friendly way. Apart from the technical difficulties in doing this, the reasoning assumes that government policy can fundamentally control economic growth. Capitalist states all have a desire for growth, since growth boosts profits. But making desire become reality is not so easy, because the market system is out of the control of any firm, however big, any country, even the USA. Since the system has its own internal logic based on the international competition for markets and the quest for profit, governments can affect what happens only to a small extent. This is graphically shown by the current economic downturn that is resolutely refusing to respond to the recipes of the capitalist experts. However, the question of compensating for the 'polluting' effect of growth projections will need to be addressed when society really is in control of the economy, i.e. in a socialist system.

Socialists and greens agree that the exploitation of the environment is linked directly to the activities of the monopoly corporations, 500 of which dominate the world economy. Is the answer, as the greens claim, to go back to societies where small local firms operate in a steady-state market system? Leaving aside the impossibility of turning back the wheel of history in this way, if such a system was created the fundamental law of the market would still apply, i.e. a need for continuous growth and an unlimited increase in production. This is because the capitalist market is anonymous and dominated by the laws of competition. Each industrialist tries to grab as large a share of the market as possible, but to do this requires cutting prices without threatening profit. The only way to achieve this is to reduce the cost of production by cutting the value of commodities, via reducing the labour time necessary to produce them in order to produce more commodities in the same length of time. To bring about such an increase in production, capital must be invested to rationalise the labour process. The only source of this capital, in the final analysis, is profit. In other words, the dynamic of the system is the constant accumulation of capital, driven by competition, and paid for by the surplus value (profit) produced in the course of production itself. This feature of the capitalist economy, analysed by Karl Marx, fundamentally undermines the proponents of the small, steady-state market economy because the absolute need will always be there for it to grow and break out of any controls on economic expansion that might be imposed by a green government. In such circumstances, monopolies would eventually emerge, as Marx predicted they would when analysing the dynamics of growth of pre-monopoly capitalism in the 19th century.

The green macro-economic programme is based on limiting the operation of the market internationally through exchange controls, limiting capital flows and speculation, and imposing import-export controls. Despite the internationalist outlook of most greens, this programme points in the opposite direction: towards a siege economy which will foster national prejudices and preclude the international co-operation needed for sustainability.

Also, the plank of the green programme to ensure international co-operation, i.e. imposing tariffs on countries that refuse to implement environmentally-friendly policies, would lead to conflict. The USA has the most to lose since it is the biggest polluter. Therefore, it would use its dominance to punish any international trade body or country that attempted to go down this path.

It might be argued that the large degree of state control necessary for a siege economy could lead to the establishment of a steady-state, environmentally-friendly society, albeit only on a national basis. However, even if a government went a long way down the road of state control, if the market remained the growth dynamic would eventually reassert itself. In these circumstances, if the state continued to stand in the way of expansion and profits, conflict would be inevitable. During the Labour government in Britain in the 1970s, there was ferocious resistance by the capitalists which included some elements plotting a coup, when prime minister Harold Wilson took half a step in the direction of a programme that had some similarities to that of the greens. In the end, a 'green' government would either have to capitulate to the demands of the market or move to abolish it. Even if an eco-capitalist siege economy could maintain itself for a period, the measures in the green programme to reduce pollution, based on market mechanisms such as eco-taxes and permits, would be inadequate. They would also lead to more inequality, contrary to the stated aims of the greens, since eco-taxes hit the poorest hardest.

The green growth agenda

Green growth proponents can be divided into two camps - those advocating 'hard' and 'soft' sustainability. Soft sustainability provides little more than a fig leaf for firms or governments to pretend they are taking some action on the environment. Backing Kyoto would fit into this pattern. The advocates of hard sustainability, on the other hand, are sincere in wanting to tackle environmental problems and, in particular, see that steady-state green policies will make it impossible to eradicate poverty in the so-called Third World. It is clear to them that even if some of the green scenarios calling for cuts in Southern consumption, from its already near subsistence level, are not implemented, the scope for redistribution of 'surplus' consumption in the North will be small.

Most advocates of green growth say that it is not possible to reduce environmental intensity sufficiently to allow the sustainable expansion of consumption using market methods. The problems with such a programme were analysed earlier, where the conclusion was reached that the market tools available are inadequate for the scale of the task of reducing environmental intensity by 90%, the minimum necessary consistent with even modest growth in the South. Furthermore, the introduction of even these weak methods would slash the profits of the multinationals, particularly in the USA, and would therefore not be implemented.

Eco-socialism

Eco-socialism is still marginalised in the green movement but as the total inability of capitalist solutions to solve environmental problems becomes more apparent, interest in it will inevitably grow. Eco-socialists share many of the criticisms made here of market-led environmentalism. At the same time, most but not all reject the possibility of growth in consumption due to assumed bio-physical limits of the earth's resources. Therefore they advocate a steady-state economy. In this context, Marx is often criticised by eco-socialists both for his ideas on 'super-abundance' and, in particular his theory of value did not encompass an environmental dimension. The issue of super-abundance will be taken up later but the other questions can be answered now. Marx's discovery of the laws of capital accumulation and expanded reproduction, discussed earlier, pointed to capitalism's need for permanent growth in order to maintain profits, an insight of great value in the green debate today. The implication of this theory is that an ecological crisis could eventually emerge under certain circumstances. In the middle of the 19th century, however, the level of pollution was a fraction of that today and a threat to sustainability on a world scale did not exist. Marx correctly argued that there were no naturally ordained barriers to plenty and abundance, in answer to Malthus' idea that generalised poverty was an inevitable and permanent feature of the human condition.

Criticisms of the labour theory of value reveal a lack of understanding of Marx's concept. The debate here concerns the calculation of economic growth in capitalist society using GNP statistics, which provides governments with an incentive to pollute, as discussed earlier. The implication is that any economic calculation based on Marx's concept of value would have a similar effect. There are two points to make. The first is that his theory of value cannot be a tool of economic calculation. Because value is only revealed in the market after the production of the commodity it is impossible to predict whether the labour time embodied in the commodity was what Marx called 'socially necessary'. Without having such knowledge in advance, value theory cannot be used for planning purposes. Secondly, since it is only revealed in the market, the concept of value will cease to have validity in a fully-developed socialist society because the market will no longer exist. It will be explained later how a socialist society could organise planning so that the 'polluting' effects of growth targets are eliminated.

The most positive aspect of the development of the eco-socialist movement is that planning is now being seriously debated as a tool to organise production, as is the possible danger of the degeneration of a future planned socialist society into a totalitarian state such as happened in the Soviet Union. This serious discussion of planning in environmental circles is a harbinger of a wider debate that will develop in the anti-capitalist movement in the next few years. However, it is important to understand the implications for future society of what many eco-socialists are saying about the requirement for massive cuts in consumption.

Some supporters of eco-socialism advocate a cut in consumption of ten times, including massive cuts in the Third World. The political form of such a society, which would have a material basis at a feudal or pre-feudal level, would be 'eco-Stalinist', a totalitarian police state that would make Stalin's Russia seem benign. To talk about such a society being based on fairness and equality is a mockery, although to be fair some of its advocates are frank enough to concede that repressive measures may be necessary. (Ironically, this nightmare regime would probably not even have sufficient resources to operate the apparatus of the police state necessary to maintain itself in power.) How such an eco-society, based on near subsistence consumption, could come about is left somewhat vague by its advocates, which is not surprising since it is hard to see who it would appeal to. The mostly unspoken perspective is that it would emerge after a collapse of the present world order, due to environmental catastrophe. Even this 'hope' is probably forlorn, however, since such a state would adopt some pre-capitalist form of organisation, corresponding to its low material base, meaning the whole rotten cycle would begin again.

5 A socialist programme for the environment

The earth is clearly on the path to ecological catastrophe. This road will be marked by, amongst many other examples, the destruction of large areas of the inhabitable globe due to global warming, the chemical degradation of the atmosphere leading to an epidemic of cancer, and bequeathing the problem of toxic waste disposal to future generations for up to 100,000 years.

The responsibility for this situation lies at the door of capitalism, a system controlled by the infamous 'hidden hand' of market forces and driven by profit. The market economy has an in-built need for permanent growth, propelled by competition and the quest for profit. At the same time, apparently paradoxically, it suffers from regular slumps in production. Both tendencies lead to waste and environmental degradation, as does the anarchic, unpredictable nature of the market economy. The alternative is a socialist society which, because it does not have the *need* for indefinate growth as capitalism, will be able to adopt, in its fully developed form, a sustainable economy based on collective ownership and democratic management. A socialist society, as well as avoiding the waste inherent in capitalism, offers the overwhelming environmental advantage of providing conscious democratic control through planning. Democracy is not mentioned here accidentally, it is essential if planning is to be run efficiently. Lack of democracy was the main reason for the ecological devastation in the bureaucratically (mis-)planned economy of the former Soviet Union.

If conscious democratic control is the key to managing the environment what are the preconditions needed to make this possible? The first, of course, is to eliminate the anarchy of the market. Just as important, is to provide the mass of the people with the ability to run society. Above all, this means giving them the time and the knowledge to be able to participate actively in decision making. This could only be done if enough leisure time is available, away from the drudgery of work, to attend meetings, and undertake educational activity and personal development. In its turn, this will only be possible if there is a transformation of economic productivity so that sufficient free time is available, something that will require big growth and investment. Although it might be argued that an alternative would be simply to cut production to such a level that enough leisure time would be freed up, the outcome would be counter-productive. Standards of living would fall, scarcity would increase and all the spare time created would be taken up in a battle to make up for the lost resources. It would set person against person and 'human nature' would quickly degenerate into the worst manifestations seen under capitalism. In Marx's phrase, "All the old crap would return". The co-operation needed, particularly internationally, to tackle the environmental crisis would be impossible.

Fredrich Engels wrote in his book, Anti-Dühring, that the realm of freedom begins where necessity ends. This means that it is necessary to satisfy all material needs in order to achieve both individual freedom and, it could be added now, the freedom to effectively intervene to avoid ecological breakdown. Marxists consider that plenty is a necessary and possible condition for the coming of a fully-developed socialist society. Removing want will eliminate the causes of inequality, exploitation and conflict, and thus lay the basis for the co-operation needed for environmental regeneration. But to do this will require growth and investment.

Most greens argue that any growth is unsustainable, never mind the amount needed to completely remove scarcity and want throughout the world. Marxists put the argument round the other way: that it is impossible to tackle environmental problems without effective international planning, a prerequisite for which is eliminating the conflict that results from scarcity. Satisfying needs does not mean that they are infinite and will continue to expand indefinitely. The basic needs for the majority of the world's population are stable, i.e. clothing, food, shelter, health-care, etc, and account for the majority of consumer expenditures. In the industrialised countries, with high pressure selling and marketing, it can appear that there is an infinite demand for the latest unnecessary gizmo. However, there is actually a trend away from conspicuous consumption among the affluent middle classes, where leisure time for personal development is increasingly being put above further consumption, as for example in California. Under socialism, as the levels of wealth of the majority rise up to these heights a similar trend will appear. Also the acquisitive habits of individuals fostered by the market economy, which are the driving force of economic behaviour in a society based on scarcity, will gradually disappear as uncertainty and worry about the future recedes and high pressure selling is removed.

These factors indicate that the possibility will exist for a gradual levelling off of consumption, albeit at a much higher level than exists today. It is impossible to define exactly what this higher, equilibrium, level of consumption will be because it will depend on a multitude of unpredictable factors, not least how quickly human psychology adjusts to the new conditions. For arguments sake, and to make the position as concrete as possible, assume that consumption under socialism will be 50% higher than the current level in the advanced industrial countries, which will provide a standard of living currently enjoyed by the middle classes in the richest capitalist country, the USA. For a harmonious, efficient, socialist system to exist, the entire population of the planet must have comparable standards of living, which means that the level of consumption in the industrialised world must apply to everyone. This requires a reduction of environmental intensity of 97% for sustainability if projections of big population increases are still used (see Appendix, example 3 for details). However, the assumption that population in the South will double will not necessarily be borne out because there is a clear relationship between falling population growth and increases in consumption, even in countries where standards of living were relatively low, such as in the former Soviet bloc.

In a democratic socialist society, as well as increases in consumption, there will be a growing sense of security and solidarity (in contrast to the former Soviet Union), which is another factor that will tend to lessen the perceived need for the 'protection' of big families. So, if current projections of population increases are not reached under socialism, the scale of the environmental problem will correspondingly fall. (Recognising that the rate of population growth may fall does not in any way endorse population control, which is advocated by some greens as a way out of the crisis. Leaving aside humanitarian considerations, such methods are counter-productive because they inevitably instil enormous hostility against the state by the very poor and will frustrate efforts to build the human solidarity necessary for the socialist project. Where such schemes have been imposed by the state they have led to near insurrection followed by collapse, as in India under Indira Ghandi in the 1970s, or passive resistance and failure as in China).

In a socialist state, the scale of the ecological challenge will also be reduced by redistribution of wealth from the super-rich, who use a disproportionate share of resources, e.g. for private jets, compared to the rest of society. Since the rich absorb 5% of output, eliminating their consumption will make a small but significant difference. While this and the possibility of lower than expected population increases will mitigate the problem of reducing pollution, the size of the task will still be huge. It will require a transformation of current patterns of energy and resource use so that environmental intensity is reduced by more than a factor of ten.

Greens may argue that such a reduction in environmental intensity is impossible and that, the increase in consumption by everyone on the planet along the lines proposed here would be unsustainable and go beyond the bio-physical limits of the globe to maintain life. It may be true that there are such natural limits, but it is impossible to say what exactly they are since this depends on the possibilities of substituting with renewables and introducing new technology to increase productivity. (There is an interesting theory developed from the Second Law of

Thermodynamics, which is popular with environmentalists, that claims to show that all human activity generates irreversible increases in 'entropy' or ecological disorder, leading eventually to environmental breakdown. Even though the idea is scientifically attractive, the empirical evidence to back it up is limited. In particular, it does not predict concretely what the limits to growth are, apart from stating that they theoretically exist.) Whether a natural limit to human resource use exists is not, however, the issue, since it is not proposed to increase consumption unsustainably, but rather to explore the possibilities of transforming resource use with socialist methods.

A socialist plan for sustainability

Environmental intensity is the key factor in trying to deal with the environmental effects of increased consumption and there are three ways a reduction in its value can be achieved. The first is changing the composition of output to less damaging products. The second is to substitute harmful economic inputs such as fossil fuels with renewable energy sources. The third is to develop new technology to increase the efficiency of the use of resources. But a fourth possibility would be to decrease the environmental intensity coefficient by changing not just the technical relations of production but also the social.

Taking each of these in turn, changing the composition of output could be done by promoting public transport and energy efficient means of transportation. Socialists do not oppose the use of private cars in principle, the question will be to develop non-polluting vehicles (e.g. powered from renewable sources and made from recycled materials). Another example is to replace air travel for most short and medium haul flights by high-speed trains, again powered by renewables. It is reactionary to propose, as most greens do, that travel should be curtailed for environmental reasons, thereby forcing people to live in a constricted geographical environment. A socialist society will encourage complete freedom of movement to foster the international solidarity needed for, among other things, environmental co-operation. It is often put forward by greens that an important way to change the composition of output is for services to replace goods because they are less energy intensive. It is true that as socialism develops people will satisfy their basic wants and turn to personal development, meaning that the service sector will become bigger than that for manufactures. However, this will only happen after a big initial increase in commodity production has laid the basis for the harmonious further development of society. The goods produced in this process could be made and used on a sustainable basis.

The second factor that is important in reducing environmental intensity is to replace harmful economic inputs - such as fossil fuels, non-recycleable materials or uranium for nuclear power - with sustainable ones. A start can be made using present solar, wind, and wave power technology and then providing investment to develop it further into more effective forms. Other, as yet undiscovered techniques, will also emerge if sufficient resources are devoted to the question, as could breakthroughs in existing approaches, such as nuclear fusion. Plastics, which are derived from fossil fuels, could largely be replaced by sustainable materials that are available now, such as high-performance ceramics. This route is held back because the investment to introduce new efficient production technology will not be made as it is more profitable in the market system to continue with plastics. The use of new technology, the third factor listed above, can increase the efficiency in the use of resources, not only by developing new and better ways of generating energy but by making the production process more energy efficient.

The fourth way to achieve environmental change is through transforming the social relations in society, from those based on private property to those centred on common ownership. Such a social system, based on need not profit, would have enormous inherent advantages from the viewpoint of saving energy. For instance, it would avoid the duplication of resources, planned obsolescence and wide-scale destruction of factories, plant and machinery in slumps, characteristic of the capitalist profit system. Eliminating these features of the system will have a significant impact in increasing the efficiency of energy usage and therefore reducing pollution. But the biggest environmental advantage of a socialist society is the ability to tackle the threats facing us using democratic planning, compared to the inevitable environmental degeneration linked to the anarchy of capitalist production.

If the figures given earlier are accepted, the scale of the task is very large, since virtually all current energy sources and non-recycleable materials will have to be replaced if environmental intensity is to be reduced by more than 90%. However, the basic human and material resources exist now to achieve this. It is a question of harnessing and developing them, something that cannot be done under conditions of capitalist anarchy. With a democratic, planned economy, a start would be made immediately to bring about the changes needed. This will be a long road because the processes of degeneration and regeneration are long term. Therefore, an environmental plan must implement significant and consistent improvements over maybe 50 years. In this time, the 90%+ reduction in environmental intensity that is needed will be gradually reached.

Where will the resources for sustainable growth come from?

It has been estimated that the cost of reaching sustainability just for greenhouse gas emissions in the USA will rise to 3% of GDP after 50 years - in present money terms $300 billion per year. As has already been pointed out, implementing this task in a capitalist system would lead to the slashing of profits and therefore would not be implemented (also planning over this time frame is impossible under capitalism). On the other hand, the resources needed to reach the goal of a tenfold decrease in energy intensity can be released by the socialist economy in the following ways:

a) The elimination of unemployment. We now have again what Marx called 'a permanent army of unemployed' in the advanced capitalist countries. In Britain at the end of the present 'boom' the real jobless rate is still nearly two million. The cost in terms of lost production and benefit payments has been estimated at £5,000 per family per year. A planned economy would be able to guarantee work for everyone, with retraining provided to make sure the new jobs are meeting the needs of people, and some of the huge amount of money saved used on environmental projects.

b) Luxury expenditure for the rich will be ended. The workers in the energy-intensive luxury goods industries (e.g. making Rolls-Royces, yachts, etc) redeployed to fulfil more general needs. The capitalist experts are always keen to point out that ending the wealth of the rich will not solve the problems of society because, however obscenely well-off they are, there are not enough of them to make a big difference. Nevertheless, the rich do consume 5% of national income which amounts to £40 billion a year in Britain, a not inconsiderable sum. Some of this could be used to begin the drive for sustainability as well as the process of transforming the national health service.

c) Ending arms spending. On a world scale the waste of resources on arms is vast, reaching nearly $1 trillion per annum at the end of the Cold War, although falling to a certain extent since. This sum represents approximately $1,000 a year for every family on the planet, an amount of money that would be a big first step in lifting the majority of the world's population out of grinding poverty. Although redeploying millions of highly-skilled arms workers, some of whom will work on renewable energy projects, will be a formidable task even for a planned economy, what is certain is that under capitalism such a transformation will never take place. This is because the reason for arms expenditure will not disappear, i.e. the hostility between rival capitalist countries and, even if it did, the market system could not plan the transfer of resources needed due to its anarchic nature.

d) Eliminating the waste of capitalism. The world is dominated by a handful of multi-national corporations which duplicate expenditure in research and development, spend unnecessarily vast sums on advertising, and design products with planned obsolescence. For example, rival drug companies spend billions on developing varieties of painkillers with marginally different effectiveness. All of this activity leads to a colossal waste of resources and energy, but is perfectly logical when profit is the motivating factor.

e) Freeing the creative power of the working class. Workers in the market system have no incentive in putting in much of their energies to help out the bosses. In a socialist society, on the other hand, it will be possible to release the creative instincts of workers because no fundamental conflict of interests will exist. Although a factor which is difficult to quantify, in the long run this will be the most significant advantage of socialism. It is often said by management theorists that the real experts in any firm when a problem needs to be solved are the workers themselves.

Even in the initial period of rapid growth under socialism, which will be ten or 15 years - short in environmental terms - real strides towards sustainability can be achieved, particularly by developing new technology. But the environment will not, and cannot, be the only priority at such a time. The international co-operation needed to achieve sustainability will depend on creating a human solidarity that can only be based on mutual prosperity. This reality answers the critics who will say that the ecological situation is too urgent and serious to brook any delay or diversion of resources to other tasks. A delay is inevitable anyway since a significant initial period of assessing the damage and carefully planning a way forward will be necessary.

6 The techniques of socialist planning

After the initial time of rapid expansion, a society will emerge where the enormous power of planning, combined with the release of human resourcefulness and energy under socialism, will enable huge steps to be taken to preserve the environment.

Since a key to achieving this success will be to introduce an efficient system of planning, this poses the question: What does it actually consist of? It is allocating resources of labour and materials for the production of goods and services for the benefit of society as a whole, rather than to make profits for the capitalists. An important point is that planning is not primarily a technical question. Rather, its success will depend on creating bodies through which the working class can democratically control production from the workplace upwards. The key element will be conscious control by working people, on a day-to-day basis, of the decisions that shape their lives.

Planning will operate at three levels: nationally and internationally; at industry or sectoral level and at the individual enterprise. Considering these in turn:

a) The overall performance of the economy will be decided at the national and international levels. There will be targets for productivity growth, investment, consumption and, of course, sustainability. These would be determined democratically by institutions created after the overthrow of capitalism. Here decisions would be taken about the priorities that society must have in the initial stages - for example, health expenditure, housing and the environment.

b) At the sectoral level it will be necessary to determine consumer demand for the goods or services of any particular industry and to organise the efficient exchange of materials with other sectors. The determination of demand will be done by obtaining information from powerful proactive consumer bodies and by using the very sophisticated tools for market research developed under capitalism. Techniques developed by the big capitalist monopolies to plan the complex movement of goods between their operations around the world - such as operational research - could be adapted to organise the movement of goods between industries, avoiding bottlenecks

c) Planning at the enterprise level. The methods mentioned in b) - ie consumer committees and market research - would also be used to determine consumer needs and preferences. It is likely that as far as enterprises making consumer products are concerned (as opposed to capital goods manufacturers) a type of market system will be retained in the transition from capitalism. This could operate through small businesses or worker co-ops, but only within the framework of a nationalised economy. If the market sector was too large it would threaten to impose its inherent inequalities onto society.

Since Marx's day, and particularly since the Russian revolution, academics have written libraries full of books about why socialism cannot work. It is only possible here to briefly respond to the key points. One of the main criticisms is that planning the efficient allocation of resources is impossible because of the vast complexity of modern industrial society where millions of economic transactions take place every day. However, most of these economic interactions are between enterprises and do not involve consumers. It is quite clear that present day multi-national firms conduct planning of a similar complexity to that required under socialism all the time. The activity of the multinationals answers a further criticism that the operation of supply and demand to determine price is the only efficient way to proceed in the exchange of goods. In their international operations, companies like General Motors simply allocate resources between countries and factories without reference to the market.

As far as planning for consumer needs is concerned the key point is that active democratic institutions should exist that can compel the planning bodies to respond to their demands. In addition to this, techniques such as market research and using the internet will make the tasks faced by future socialist planners far easier than for their counterparts in the young Soviet Union. It is important, though, not to exaggerate the role that will be played by the internet or look for a 'technical fix'. The existence of democratic institutions will be paramount. The role of democratically-elected and powerful consumer bodies will also make sure that shoddy goods are not produced and quality is maintained. Here as well, the advances in modern production management techniques can be applied. Unlike the Soviet Union, the future socialist society will inherit an industrial tradition, or culture, associated with the highest levels of technique developed by capitalism.

Planning and the environment

Democratic, rational planning will permit a consistent improvement in ecological conditions to be achieved over many decades until full sustainability is reached. Above all, the condition of the environment will not be subject to the whim of the capitalist market, where it will always have a low priority. Of the three sectors of a socialist economy mentioned above, the most important for the environment is the first - that is - planning at the national and particularly international level. Here it will be a question of the direct allocation of resources to fulfil improvements that have been democratically agreed in all countries. The planning bodies will organise the progressive replacement of fossil fuel energy sources with renewables and the elimination of non-recyclable materials. Investment will be directed to low environmentally-intensive sectors, such as public transport, and to research aimed at promoting sustainability. That could include new non-polluting energy sources for private transportation or electricity generation.

In the broader economy it will be necessary, when setting planned growth targets, to make sure that the costs of environmental damage are not included in the definition of 'growth', as happens under capitalism. This can be simply done by adapting a current technique that measures a 'sustainability gap'. This indicates, in physical terms that can be used by a planner, the degree of consumption which is in excess of that required for sustainability. The sustainability gap indicators are related to different economic sectors so that the key areas to focus on are identified. This could then form the basis of targets to be built into the plan.

In the transition to a fully-developed socialist economy the consumer goods sector will still be regulated through price mechanisms operating in a type of market system. This raises the question; Should consumer behaviour be encouraged to change in an environmentally-friendly way by market mechanisms, e.g. increasing the tax on petrol? The most important point to make, as discussed above, is that the key to sustainability lies in implementing policies at the international and national level - to adopt wind, wave or solar power, for example. It will not be necessary to increase taxes on petrol to pay for this, since sufficient resources will be created by the democratically- planned system. It is true that consumer behaviour is sensitive to price - for example, in the choice between private and public transport. But a subsidy to the latter, designed both to cut fares and boost capacity, would have a more positive effect on behaviour than a tax rise on fuel. It would also be fairer, because taxes on fuel tend to hit the poorest hardest. This will especially be the situation in Southern countries that are rapidly developing under socialism, but where the costs of heating and cooking still form a large proportion of living expenses.

Other keys to ecological transformation, such as developing new technology, will be achieved by direct allocation of investment. Market mechanisms will at most play a marginal role in an Environmental plan, although some techniques that have been developed, such as, cost-benefit analysis when stripped of the distortions found when applied in a capitalist context, could be useful.

Input-output analysis

Planning tools already developed for national capitalist economies or multi-national companies can be adapted for the environment. These could be marketing techniques used to predict consumer behaviour or tools to allocate resources. The most useful and powerful of these is input-output analysis, created by Vassily Leontief, on the basis of his work at the state planning body, Gosplan, in the Soviet Union in the 1920s. Leontief came to the West in the 1930s and applied his idea to firms and national economies, particularly the USA. (In the post-war economic boom, when conditions were relatively stable, it appeared that his technique was useful in predicting economic performance and fitted in with the reformist idea, popular at the time, of planning market systems.)

Input-output analysis determines the relations between the major branches of a national economy. Leontief's original input-output table refers to eleven branches of industry plus agriculture, transport and households. It takes the form of a matrix with the branches arranged horizontally and vertically. The horizontal rows show what each of the 14 branches sells to the 13 others, while the vertical columns show what resources each branch buys from the others. As a simple starting point, assume that the relations between different branches remain stable, e.g. an increase in steel production of 10% needs an increase of 10% in coke supplied by another branch. Technical coefficients can in this way be worked out between all branches of production, up to virtually any number, and can be of a very complex nature - easily handled, however, by computers. The result is that predictions can be made about what resources will be needed to fulfil a particular requirement of the plan.

In the 1970s, Leontief further developed his system to include environmental

Leontief's Input-Output Table for Environmental Planning

Outputs \ Inputs	Economy	Environment
Economy	*1*	*3*
Environment	*2*	*4*

resources. A simplified input-output table is drawn above that shows the interrelationship of economic and environmental systems. Square 1 shows the interdependence between the sectors of the economy e.g. consumption, capital investment, etc. and final demand. Square 2 contains the environmental outputs that are used as inputs to the different economic sectors (e.g. raw materials, water) or which go directly to final demand without having been used in production (e.g. oxygen).

Square 3 is the output of the economic system into the environment, that is the emissions occurring in production and consumption. If the sectors are considered separately, squares 2 and 3 indicate the environmental inputs by sector and the sectoral sources of emissions respectively.

Such a dis-aggregation of the environment - seperating it into ground, water and air systems - shows from which system natural resources come and to which sectors of the environment emissions go. Finally, square 4 contains flows among branches of the environment. The technique will permit, for example, an estimation of the quantity of pollutants (in tonnes) that are generated by a certain level of consumer demand. The simple system described here can be expanded and developed to include a complex set of relationships linking all environmental and economic factors to become a powerful planning tool.

Lessons from the Soviet Union

The Soviet Union was the world's first workers' state and at its beginning was a beacon for all the poor and downtrodden throughout the planet. However, by the time of its collapse more than ten years ago, it had not only failed economically, it was also a byword for ecological devastation. Massive regions of Central Asia were made deserts by unsustainable intensive agriculture, and the Aral Sea - one of the earth's biggest inland water sources - virtually ceased to exist. Toxic air and water pollution had reached such extremes that whole areas were uninhabitable, with the picture being completed by the world's worst nuclear disaster in 1986 at Chernobyl in Ukraine. Such evidence, critics will argue, shows that even if the socialist programme put forward here seems plausible, the experience of 'actual existing socialism' in the Soviet Union proved otherwise.

It would, however, be wrong to describe the Soviet Union as socialist in any way, apart from in its early years. Real socialism must be based on both a planned economy and active, democratic bodies controlling all aspects of society, including harmonising the needs of producers, consumers and the environment. (Under capitalism there will always be antagonism between them.) Democratic bodies are needed, not for abstract reasons, but as the essential mechanism that will decide how to allocate resources efficiently and in an environmentally-friendly way. Leon Trotsky, one of the main leaders of the Russian revolution, described the Soviet Union as a 'bureaucratically deformed workers' state'. He explained that although capitalism had been overthrown, and that technically society belonged to the working class, it was actually in the grip of bureaucrats who had destroyed all vestiges of democracy and who ruled to preserve their own interests.

This totalitarian dictatorship came about in the mid-1920s when Stalin moved to crush all the elements of workers' democracy that were established by the October 1917 revolution that overthrew capitalism. This was possible because the country was devastated by years of imperialist war and externally imposed civil conflict, and was persecuted and isolated as the only workers' state in the world. In these circumstances of total impoverishment, the priority for the vast majority of the population was the struggle to survive. Such a situation inevitably cut across popular participation in the running of the economy and society, creating the conditions for a new elite to develop, together with remnants of the pre-revolutionary regime. The new layer in society, represented politically by Stalin, aimed to secure for themselves the lion's share of small resources that were available. Trotsky described how, when allocating scarce food, it was the bureaucrats who ate first and best. He demonstrated that the growth of the privileged elite that subsequently strangled the Soviet Union originated in the conditions of scarcity existing at the time. Yet, even in this terrible situation, political degeneration was not inevitable, because a successful workers' revolution in a richer country - something that did not turn out but was possible - would have lent the Soviet Union the material support it needed to survive as a viable socialist state.

Despite the huge dead weight round its neck due to the bureaucrats, the Soviet Union grew at rates unprecedented anywhere, before or since, due to the advantages of planning. This was, however, at a cost of staggering waste and environmental destruction due to the mismanagement and indifference of the new ruling caste. Like their capitalist counterparts, the new rulers had no reason to consider the effect of industrialisation on the environment because their focus was purely on enriching themselves.

When socialism is established in the future, it is extremely unlikely that a Stalinist degeneration would happen again, because the situation in Russia in the 1920s was so overwhelmingly unfavourable due to a unique combination of circumstances. This was recognised by Lenin and Trotsky, the leaders of the revolution, who had a perspective of holding on until help came from the workers in the West. It is much more likely that the next socialist society will begin from a point much closer to the standard of living of the advanced capitalist countries, as originally envisaged by Marx. Also the lessons of Stalinism have been learnt, which will lead to increased vigilance to prevent any vestige of bureaucratic degeneration developing. Lenin understood this danger and proposed that no Soviet official should receive more than the average workers' wage, and that elected representatives should be subject to immediate recall and replacement. Similar rules will be necessary in a future socialist society as a guarantee against any repeat of the past.

A programme for sustainable growth.

A long-term programme of investment in renewable energy sources must be a priority, leading to the progressive replacement of oil, gas, coal-fired and nuclear power stations. Workers in these industries would need to be retrained and reskilled for the different technologies involved in wind, wave and solar power generation.

At the same time, research and development in new techniques for energy generation would be massively stepped up, along with work to improve the capability and efficiency of presently available renewable energy sources. The extra experts needed to do this work could be assigned from the arms industry, a sector which would be rapidly run down. Significant resources will still need to be deployed to clearing up the mess already existing. In particular, workers in the nuclear industry will have their hands full in organising decommissioning nuclear plant and devising ways to safely store or neutralise toxic waste.

Environmentally-friendly consumption habits can be promoted by giving subsidies to key areas, such as public transport and the use of recycleable materials. In general, eco-taxes, which hit the poorest hardest, should not be used unless directed at certain items of energy intensive luxury consumption. Enterprises should be subject to a strict regime of compliance with environmental standards.

To implement this programme would require an integrated environmental plan that can only be effective if the energy industries are nationalised with democratic workers' control and management. The research and development investment required for ecological transformation can also only be effective if it is part of an integrated plan, linked to other aspects such as energy production and consumer subsidies.

Since the issues of environmental sustainability involve virtually all aspects of production of goods and services, an integrated energy plan must be part of an overall plan, which can only be based on taking over the key sectors of the economy. This means nationalising, under democratic workers' control and management, the top 500 monopolies that dominate the world. If this were done the anarchy and waste built into the capitalist system could be eliminated. On that basis a rational socialist alternative could begin the task of saving the planet from its present path towards devastation.

Background Reading

- *Scientific Basis for the Greenhouse Effect,* by WR Cline, *Economic Journal,* No 101, July 1991, pp904-19
- *Economic Growth and Environmental Sustainability, The Prospects for Green Growth,* by Paul Ekins, Routledge, 2000
- *Economic Growth Versus the Environment,* by R Lecomber, Macmillan, 1975
- *Economics of the Environment: Theory and Policy,* by Horst Siebert, 4th edition, Springer, 1995
- *Eco-Socialism,* by David Pepper, Routledge, 1993
- *Eco-Socialism or Eco-Capitalism,* by Saral Sarkar, Zed Books, 1999
- *Energy and the Environment,* by R A Ristinen and J J Kraushaar, Wiley, 1999
- *Counting the Cost of Global Warming,* by J Broome, White Horse Press, Cambridge, 1992
- *Global Warning. Socialism and the Environment,* by Martin Cock and Bill Hopwood, Militant Publications, 1996
- *Green Economics,* by Molly Scott Cato and Miriam Kennett, Green Audit, 1999
- *History of Environmental Economic Thought,* by E Kula, Routledge, 1998
- *The North, the South and the Environment,* edited by V Bhaskar and A Glynn, Earthscan, 1995
- *Planning Sustainability,* edited by M Kenny and J Meadowcroft, Routledge, 1999
- *Steady State Economics,* by H E Daly, Earthscan, 1992

Appendix

The Commoner-Erlich Equation

Barry Commoner, the well-known environmental writer and theorist, first developed the equation in the 1970s, later modified into the form I = PCT. In this formula, I is the environmental impact, P is population, C is consumption per head, and T is the environmental impact per unit of consumption. The implication of this formula, taken at face value, is that increases in personal consumption and population will increase the (negative) environmental impact. However, if T (also known as the Environmental Impact Coefficient, EIC, or environmental intensity) is reduced at the same time as P and C are going up, the negative effects of these increases can be mitigated.

Calculations using the Commoner-Erlich Equation. (Source: Ekins 2000)
The equation has the form: I = PCT

If we assume:
p^H is the population in the advanced capitalist, high-income countries, p^L the equivalent figure in low-income countries, c^H the consumption per head in the high-income countries, c^L the consumption figure for low-income areas

Then:
$I = [p^H.c^H + p^L.c^L]\ T$
At the moment $p^H = 902$ million, $c^H = \$24,930$, $p^L = 4,771$ million, $c^L = \$1,090$ million,

Therefore: $I = [902 \times 24,930 + 4,771 \times 1,090]\ T$

Rearranging the equation gives the current value of environmental impact per unit of consumption:
$T = I/\ [902.10^6 \times 24,930 + 4771.10^6 \times 1,090] = I/27.69 \times 10^{12}$

Now consider the three cases mentioned in the main article:

1. If there is no growth in population or consumption and it is assumed that I must be reduced by 50% for sustainability, then it is clear from the equation that T must also be reduced by the same amount, i.e. 50%.

2. If there is a factor of four growth in consumption per head, the population of the high-income countries rises to 1,186 million and the low-income countries to 10,160 million: If the environmental impact is reduced by 50%, then the new value of T needed for sustainability will be:
$Tnew = 0.5 \times I/[1,186.10^6 \times 4 \times 24,930 + 10,160.10^6 \times 4 \times 1090] = 0.5 \times I/162.6 \times 10^{12}$

Dividing this figure by the current estimate for T made above gives:
Tnew = 0.09 x T. Therefore, T must be reduced by 91% for sustainability.

3. If the population rises as in example 2 above, and consumption for the entire world is 50% higher that currently found in the industrialised countries then the new value of T for sustainability will be:
   Tnew = 0.5 x I/[11,346.10^6 x 1.5 x 24,930] = I/8.5 x 10^{14}

   Dividing this figure by the current estimate for T made above gives:
   Tnew = 0.033 x T. Therefore, T must be reduced by 97% for sustainability.

How reliable are these predictions and where did they come from? Firstly, is a 50% reduction in environmental impact necessary for sustainability? The first point that needs to be made is that the Commoner-Erlich equation must be applied to each source of pollution separately. To aggregate the results over many disparate environmental threats would produce very arbitrary results. However, to take the example of global warming, the most serious problem of all, the Intergovernmental Panel on Climate Change (IPCC) said that CO2 emissions need to be cut by 60% to stabilise its concentration in the atmosphere. Other greenhouse gasses need to be cut by an average of more than 70% according to the IPCC. These statistics indicate that a 50% reduction in environmental impact is a conservative figure to use in predicting the conditions for sustainability due to global warming.

A complicating factor in applying the equation is that it assumes that there is no relationship between the variables of P, C and T. However, it has been claimed, using the USA as an example, that intensity in the use of resources (T) falls with rising consumption per head. This would tend to increase the cut in the environmental impact (I) needed for sustainability, compared to the case where the variables are assumed not to be related. Other examples could be given which bend the results in the opposite direction. Also it is important to separate the calculations for the 'North' and the 'South' because their levels of consumption are vastly different.

Contacting the CWI

The Committee for a Workers' International has affiliated parties and organisations in more than 35 countries on all continents. The way to contact our comrades differs from country to country. Some you can contact directly. For others, it is easier to do it via the CWI offices in London... e-mail to the International Office of the CWI: inter@dircon.co.uk or contact us at PO Box 3688, London, E11 1YE, UK. Telephone: + 44 (0)20 8558 5814. Fax: + 44 (0)20 8988 8793. Our website is on: http://www.worldsocialist-cwi.org

If you want to know more about us in... Cyprus, Finland, Kashmir, Pakistan or anywhere else...then contact the CWI international offices above.

Australia: Socialist Party.
PO Box 1015, Collingwood, Victoria 3066.
phone: + 61 3 9650 0160;
e-mail: sp@mira.net
Austria: Sozialistische Linkspartie.
Kaiserstrasse 14/11, 1070 Wien.
phone: + 43 1 524 6310;
fax: + 43 1 524 6311; e-mail: slp@slp.at
Belgium: LSP/MA. PO Box10, 1190 Vorst 3;
phone: + 322 3456181;
e-mail: lspmas@skynet.be
Brazil: Socialismo Revolucionario. Caixa Postal 02009, CEP 01060-970, Sao Paulo S.P. phone: + 55 11 339 5684
e-mail: sr-cio@uol.com.br
Britain: Socialist Party. PO Box 24697, London, E11 1YD. phone: + 44 (0)20 8988 8777; fax: + 44 (0)20 8988 8787;
e-mail: campaigns@socialistparty.org
Canada: Socialist Alternative. 903-633 Bay Street, Toronto, Ontario, MSG 2G4
e-mail: socialistalternative@canada.com
Chile: Celso C Campos, Casilla 50310, Correo Central, Santiago.
phone: + 56 2 622 9004;
e-mail: jandresverra@hotmail.com
CIS: 125167 Moscow a\Ya 37, Moscow.
e-mail: pabgem@online.ru
Czech Republic: Socialistická Alternativa - Budoucnost.
D.V.S., PO Box 227, Bubenské nábřeží 306, 170 05 Praha 7-Holešovice
e-mail: budoucnost@email.cz
France: Les amis de L'Egalite.
Centre 166, 82 rue Jeanne d'Arc, 76000 Rouen. e-mail: grcontact@hotmail.org
Germany: Sozialistische Alternative.
Litten Straße. 106/107, 10179 Berlin.
phone: + 49 302 47 23 802;
e-mail: bundsleitung@sav-online.de
Greece: Xekinima.
8 Gortynos Street, PO Box 11254 Athens.
phone/fax: + 30 1 524 7177;
e-mail: xekinima@hotmail.com
India: Dudiyora Horaata.
PO Box 1828, Bangalore 560018.
e-mail: dudiyorahoraata@usnl.net
Ireland North: Socialist Party.
2nd Floor, 36 Victoria Square, Belfast BT1.
phone: + 44 (0)2890 232962;
fax: + 44 (0)2890 311778;
e-mail: socialist@belfastsp.freeserve.co.uk
Ireland South: Socialist Party.
PO Box 3434, Dublin 8.
phone/fax: + 353 1 677 25 92;
e-mail: info@socialistparty.net
Israel/Palestine: Maavak Sozialisti.
e-mail: info@maavak.org.il
Japan: CWI Japan. Urbain Higashi Mikuni 9-406, Higashi-Mikuni 2-10, Yadokawa-ku, Osaka-shi. phone/fax: + 81 6 396 6998;
e-mail: nixsc@dion.ne.jp
Netherlands: Offensief.
PO Box 11561, 1001 GN Amsterdam.
e-mail: info@offensief.nl
New Zealand:
e-mail: Nz_tin_bowron@hotmail.com
Nigeria: Democratic Socialist Movement.
PO Box 2225, Agege, Lagos.
tel: +234 1492 5671
e-mail: dsm@beta.linkserve.com
Portugal: Alternativa Socialista.
Apartado 27018, 1201-950, Lisboa
e-mail: Alternativa_socialista@clix.pt
Scotland: CWI. PO Box 6773, Dundee, DD1 1YL. phone: + 44 141 221 7714;
South Africa: Democratic Socialist Movement. PO Box 596, Newton, 2113, Johannesburg. phone: + 27 11 342 2220;
e-mail: democraticsocialist@mweb.co.za
Spain: Manifiesto.
Apd. de correos 4435, CP41001, Sevilla
email: meurig@altavista.net
Sri Lanka: United Socialist Party.
261/1 Kirula Road, Narahempito, Colombo 5. phone: + 94 1 508 821
e-mail: usp@wow.lk
Sweden: Rattvisepartiet Socialisterna.
PO Box 73; 123 03 Farsta. phone: + 46 8 605 9400. fax: + 46 8 556 252 52;
e-mail: rs@socialisterna.org
USA: Socialist Alternative.
PO Box 45343, Seatlle, W4, 98145.
e-mail: info@socialistalternative.org